FOOD FOR THOUGHT

... *taste and see*

Food for Thought

...taste and see

Meditational Reflections
and
Inspirational Insights
from the
Outpourings of My Soul

By Henry Manley

Food for Thought

... taste and see

By Henry Manley

Copyright © 2018 Rose Marie Manley

No part of this book may be reproduced in any form or by any means, electronic or mechanical, including photocopying, recording, or by storage and retrieval system, without written permission from The Laurus Company, Inc. and the author.

ISBN 978-1-943523-48-1 Paperback Book
ISBN 978-1-943523-49-8 Kindle
ISBN 978-1-943523-50-4 ePub (iBooks, Nook)

Published by LAURUS BOOKS

LAURUS BOOKS
www.TheLaurusCompany.com

Laurus Books is an imprint of The Laurus Company, Inc.

This book may be ordered in paperback from: TheLaurusCompany.com, Amazon.com, BarnesandNoble.com, Spring Arbor, and other retailers around the world. Check for availability in formats for electronic readers from their respective stores.

Meditational Reflections
and
Inspirational Insights
from the
Outpourings of My Soul

– Henry Manley

DEDICATION

The writings contained in this project are in memory of
my mother who is now deceased.

Nellie C. Manley

I was fortunate enough to have had a conversation with her the morning prior to her departure. One of her requests was that I complete this project. I promised her that I would.

She was a devout believer and follower of the Lord Jesus Christ, a woman of integrity and one of great faith. She dedicated her life to serving God by serving others.

Her many achievements, if I were to list them all, would contain more than a volume of books within themselves.

I am grateful to have known such a Great Soul!

FOOD FOR THOUGHT … *taste and see*

THE INNOCENCE OF MY YOUTH

Innocence, the companion of my youth,
you were my prize possession.
Where have you gone?
Where are the days of joy and laughter?
How did you elude my grasp?
I have sought for you everywhere,
in the high places and in the low places,
only to realize that among the shadows of death,
the creatures of the night,
that my innocence has been stolen.
Oh, lover of my soul!
I cry out for you
in the dark nights of human experience
—where are you?
My innocence is gone; it is no longer with me.
Only your light divine can restore unto me
that which my soul seeks to find …
THE INNOCENCE OF MY YOUTH.

FOOD FOR THOUGHT ... *taste and see*

TIME

Time is a measurement of moments
birthed out of the realm of eternity.
It is like a precious commodity
once consumed can never be retrieved.
Be cautious on how it's spent,
for therein lies the true purpose for living
imbedded in a capsule of time.

DIVINE JUSTICE

When operating in a carnal mindset,
it inhibits the ability to remain neutral
when wronged or offended.
Revenge or resentment will always appear to be
a natural course of reaction to an offense or wrong.
Carnality causes spiritual blindness
that prohibits the ability to see the hand of God
operating in the laws of reciprocation and retribution,
balancing the scales of justice.
In the words of this truth
we come to understand the revelation of God's word:
"Vengeance is mine, I will repay."
For the soul that truly comprehends this truth,
forgiving offenses is no longer an option;
it becomes a condition for ensuring eternal life.

FOOD FOR THOUGHT ... *taste and see*

LIFE

Stained and spotted
by the blemishes we bring to life,
the precious source of all existence.
It is not how life treats us
but how we treat life
that determines our success in it.

FOOD FOR THOUGHT ... *taste and see*

LOVING THE UNLOVABLE

Pure unconditional love
is a gift bestowed upon mankind by God.
It transcends
human expressions of love
based upon reward.
It is the essence
of His nature, revealed through Christ
and imputed to us by His Spirit
that enables and empowers us
to love the unlovable.

FOOD FOR THOUGHT ... *taste and see*

FAITH

Through the benevolence of God,
every soul is given a measure of faith;
the ability to believe that God is.
However,
trusting in Him
is another matter the soul must resolve
in order to please him.

FOOD FOR THOUGHT ... *taste and see*

THE HEART

Just as surely as the night sky is filled with darkness,
so is the heart of man desperately wicked.
For out of the heart spring forth
all sorts of malign designs,
which are only the effect of the root cause
that lies hidden in dark chambers
of the heart.
More often than not, these designs reveal
who we really are.

FOOD FOR THOUGHT ... *taste and see*

WORDS

Words.
They can inspire the mind and motivate the heart.
Words.
They are like fire, exciting passion in the soul.
Words.
They can corrupt communication, distorting reality.
Words.
They are like arrows, propelled by the bow of desire,
armed with aim, purpose, design, and function.

TO KNOW HIM

To know who we are in Christ
gives us a powerful sense
of identity and belongingness.
But, to know who He is in us
overwhelms the soul
with the security of His Love.

FOOD FOR THOUGHT ... *taste and see*

AWARENESS

Knowledge is awareness.
Wisdom is the right application of awareness.
Understanding is comprehension of the
purpose of awareness.

FOOD FOR THOUGHT ... *taste and see*

YOUR PRESENCE

When I looked upon your face the first time,
I saw you, and our presence merged.
I realized there was a fire emanating from your eyes
that ignited passion in my soul;
it heightened the beat of my heart as if to explode!
Only discipline and containment enabled me
to maintain my mental and emotional equilibrium.

FOOD FOR THOUGHT ... *taste and see*

YOUR SMILE

Your smile
is like a moment in eternity.
It never changes.
It can warm the coldness of hearts.
When it rains, hails or snows,
or even when the wind blows,
it never moves out of place
on your beautiful face.

FOOD FOR THOUGHT ... *taste and see*

THE FRAGRANCE OF YOUR BEAUTY

The fragrance of your beauty is intoxicating.
If it were wine that I could drink,
I would be drunk for days.
Like a spider that weaves its web to catch its prey,
so has your beauty and charm
ensnared and captured my heart.
I surrender!

FOOD FOR THOUGHT ... *taste and see*

KNOWING

It is not how much we know
but what we become
as a result of what we do know
that matters.

FOOD FOR THOUGHT ... *taste and see*

THE ANOINTED ONE

Blessed be the Christ,
the Anointed One.
You are the Lover of my soul
in Whom I put my trust.
You are the Nourisher and
Sustainer of my life.
It is through Your maternal love
that I am fed
Your life-sustaining word.

IN HIS IMAGE AND LIKENESS

God created us in His image and
allows us to indulge in human experience
in order to test us to see
who is best in conduct and who will obey Him,
that He may develop in us
His likeness
through human experience.

FOOD FOR THOUGHT ... *taste and see*

A SONG OF CONFESSION

O LORD!
We have succumbed to the allurements of sin and
have been found guilty by virtue of
thoughts and committed acts.
We beseech you, Lord, for forgiveness, and
we pray for your mercy and grace to be granted unto us
to endure the consequences of our sin.
Amen.

FOOD FOR THOUGHT ... *taste and see*

FLATTERY

Flattery is like sweet chocolate;
it goes down real smooth.
Its words are like red wine;
they intoxicate the mind.
Flattery's deadly import of deceit
meanders its way into the heart
where its message is planted for a season,
waiting to manifest for a reason.

FOOD FOR THOUGHT ... *taste and see*

PURPOSE

When potential and purpose
are aligned together,
they provide vision and direction
for the fulfillment of destiny.

FOOD FOR THOUGHT ... *taste and see*

THE FOLLY OF ENVY AND OWNERSHIP

The earth and its fullness belong to the Creator.
So why fret over another's portion
when God has rendered to all men
their portion in the earth.
Be diligent to plant your seed and
tend to your own soil.
In time you, too, will realize a harvest.
At the end of this earthly journey,
all that was given in exchange for human effort
must return to its rightful owner,
"GOD."

FOOD FOR THOUGHT ... *taste and see*

ENTICEMENT

Beware, my Friend!
Be diligent to guard your heart.

Beware, my Friend!
Catchy clichés are on the loose.

Beware, my Friend!
They are always loaded with seeds of enticement.

FOOD FOR THOUGHT ... *taste and see*

THE METAMORPHOSIS OF REVELATION

Revelation is found embedded
within the core of a seed of thought,
which brings forth illumination
that gives birth to inspiration,
which brings about motivation
that ultimately leads to materialization.

FOOD FOR THOUGHT ... *taste and see*

MEDIOCRITY

OH, MEDIOCRITY!
You are like a diamond-studded crown
with cubic zirconia in its setting.
You obscure the soul's vision of excellence,
and the unfortunate heart
that is motivated by your presence
shall become impoverished
in times of famine and drought.

FOOD FOR THOUGHT ... *taste and see*

CHANGING REALITIES

When the storms of life divert our attention
away from God,
the line of conscious communication with Him
becomes broken.
When this state of being occurs,
our perception changes to self-consciousness,
ultimately changing our realities.
In this state,
we are no longer walking in the spirit of truth.

FOOD FOR THOUGHT ... *taste and see*

HUMAN ORACLE

The human soul
was designed by its Creator
to be an oracle
for expression of love and truth
in the earth.

FOOD FOR THOUGHT ... *taste and see*

MERCY

It is God's unmerited mercy toward us
that operates in the earth for our good.
It is His mercy that beckons us
to the path of grace
when we have fallen away
from its guiding light.

FOOD FOR THOUGHT ... *taste and see*

GRACE

Our lives
are predicated on purpose and its grace,
God's divine favor
that brings purpose into realization in our lives.
Its grace,
God's enabling power
that empowers us to perform the will of God for our lives.
This is our portion
assigned to us before the foundation of the world
in the mind of God.

ABOUT THE AUTHOR

HENRY MANLEY

HENRY MANLEY attended Elizabeth City State University for three and a half years until he left to start up a new tax business. He later graduated from Cayuga Community College where he majored in Business. After graduating, he ran his successful tax business for 35 years. Being versatile in nature, Mr. Manley counseled people about their taxes, helped them get houses, create wills, etc. He is now retired.

Mr. Manley has been married to Rose Manley for 27 years at the time of this writing. He has one son who is a doctor. His wife has a son and a daughter.

He is a born again believer and serves God by serving man. He is a member of Deeper Life Ministries in Little Washington, North Carolina, pastored by William and Dorothy Guilford.

www.ingramcontent.com/pod-product-compliance
Lightning Source LLC
Chambersburg PA
CBHW070857050426
42453CB00012B/2252